FIRST
LOOK AT

KEEPING WARM

For a free color catalog describing Gareth Stevens' list of high-quality children's books, call 1-800-341-3569 (USA) or 1-800-461-9120 (Canada).

Library of Congress Cataloging-in-Publication Data

Baker, Susan, 1961-
    First look at keeping warm / Susan Baker.
      p. cm. — (First look)
    "North American edition"—T.p. verso.
    Includes bibliographical references and index.
    Summary: Describes the different ways animals and people protect themselves from cold
weather and discusses how body heat, food, shelter, sunshine, clothing, and fuels all work
to keep us warm.
    ISBN 0-8368-0704-9
    1. Body temperature—Regulation—Juvenile literature. [1. Body temperature—Regulation.]
I. Title. II. Series.
QP135.B25 1991
591.1'88—dc20   91-9423

North American edition first published in 1991 by

Gareth Stevens Children's Books
1555 North RiverCenter Drive, Suite 201
Milwaukee, Wisconsin 53212, USA

U.S. edition copyright © 1991 by Gareth Stevens, Inc. First published as *Keeping Warm*
in the United Kingdom, copyright © 1991, by Simon & Schuster Young Books.
Additional end matter copyright © 1991 by Gareth Stevens, Inc.

Photograph credits: Martyn Chillmaid, 29; Bruce Coleman, cover, 6, 7, 9, 10, 18, 27;
Sally and Richard Greenhill, 13, 14, 16, 17, 19, 26; ZEFA, all others

Series editor: Patricia Lantier-Sampon
Design: M&M Design Partnership
Cover design: Laurie Shock
Layout: Sharone Burris

Printed in the United States of America

1 2 3 4 5 6 7 8 9 97 96 95 94 93 92 91

FIRST
LOOK AT

SUSAN BAKER

KEEPING WARM

Gareth Stevens Children's Books

MILWAUKEE

Books in the
FIRST LOOK series:

CONTENTS

FUR AND FEATHERS

What keeps birds and other animals warm in cold weather?

Have you ever noticed what happens to a squirrel's coat in winter? Why do you think birds fluff out their feathers on a cold day?

7

SHELTER FROM THE STORM

Farmers bring some of their animals in from the cold, but sheep can live outdoors in all kinds of weather. How do sheep stay warm in winter?

Can you think of some places where wild animals and birds find shelter?

9

WINTER WOOLLIES

People use sheep's wool and sheepskin to make warm clothes.

How do you think these people's clothes were made?

Have you ever tried knitting or weaving?

11

12

HOT FOOD AND DRINK

Your body burns up the food you eat, making heat and energy, just like a fire burning fuel.

A hot drink warms you up quickly. Which part of your body feels hot first?

HEALTHY EXERCISE

Food gives you energy to run and jump and play exciting games.

How do you feel after you have been skipping or running hard?

Why do you think people sweat?

WARM WORK

Hard work like digging can warm you
up on a cold day.

Some workplaces are very warm.
Can you think of some ways that people
protect themselves from the heat?

17

SUNSHINE

What do you like doing in the Sun?

Do you start shivering after you have been swimming?

How do you get warm again?

19

WRAPPING UP

What kinds of clothes do you wear in cold weather? Do certain types of clothes keep you warmer than others? Which clothes keep you dry?

Do you ever feel too hot in stores or on buses? Why do you think this happens?

HOME SWEET HOME

When it is cold, wet, and windy, people either take shelter or hurry home where it is warm and dry.

Which parts of a house help keep the rain, wind, and snow away?

23

FIRES AND FUEL

You can get as warm as toast near an open fire. What is the fire screen for? How is your home heated?

How do you think these hunters are able to keep warm while they are sleeping and working outdoors?

COZY CORNERS

Do you like to find a warm spot to curl up in and read? What are your favorite places?

What do pets do to keep themselves warm?

BEDTIME

You burn up only a small amount of energy when you are quiet or asleep.

Bed sheets and blankets trap air and keep it close to your skin. The heat of your body warms up the air.

How does it feel when you go to bed and snuggle down under thick, light covers?

29

More Books about Keeping Warm

All about Wool. Jobin (Young Discovery Library)
Animal Homes (2 vols.) Crump (National Geographic)
Animals in the Cold. Carwardine (Garrett Educational Corporation)
Clementine's Winter Wardrobe. Spohn (Franklin Watts)
Exercise: What It Is, What It Does. Trier (Greenwillow)
Heat. Jennings (Childrens Press)
Hot and Cold. Ardley (Franklin Watts)
Hot and Cold. Pluckrose (Franklin Watts)
Sweater. Tippell (Silver Burdett)
What Happens When You Run? Richardson (Gareth Stevens)
When Winter Comes. Freedman (Dutton)

Glossary

Energy: Power that is used to make machines run or to help people work or play. The Sun, oil, and water provide the world with most of its energy. People can get energy from the foods they eat.

Exercise: Any activity that can help keep a person's body in good health. Swimming, running, bicycling, and hiking are good exercises that are also fun.

Fire screen: A special device made of metal netting attached to a frame that is placed in front of open fires or fireplaces. Fire screens help protect people from sparks that may fly out of a fire as it burns.

Fuel: Any material or substance that is burned or used to produce heat or power.

Fur: The soft, thick hair that covers many animals. Rabbits, bears, foxes, cats, and squirrels are a few animals that have fur.

Knitting: A type of sewing that is done with special needles and thread or yarn. Wool sweaters for cold-weather wear can be knitted either by hand or by machine.

Sheepskin: A special type of leather that is made from the skin of a sheep. Sheepskin clothing is very warm, so the material is good for cold temperatures.

Sweat: To perspire; to work or play so hard that small drops of water or moisture form and collect on the outside of the skin. People and animals can sweat just by sitting out in the Sun.

Weaving: Making cloth by crisscrossing strands of thread or yarn in and around each other on a special device called a loom.

Winter: The season of the year between autumn and spring. Winter weather gets very extreme as one moves away from the equator and closer to the poles. Many animals hibernate during winter.

Wool: The soft, curly hair that covers some animals, such as sheep. Wool is used to make clothing for people who live in cold places.

Index

A number that is in **boldface** type means that the page has a picture of the subject on it.